ЭТА КНИГА ПРИНАДЛЕЖИТ

This book belongs to

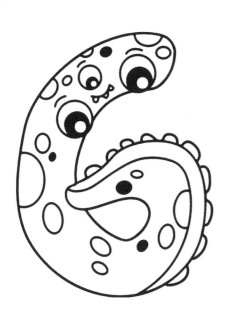

First Russian Words Coloring Book: Numbers, Colors, Shapes.

Первые Слова, Раскраска: Цифры. Цвета. Формы.

ЦИФРЫ

[tsifry]   numbers

First Russian Words Coloring Book: Numbers, Colors, Shapes.

Первые Слова, Раскраска: Цифры. Цвета. Формы.

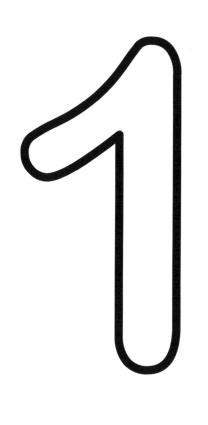

ОДИН
[odin]   one

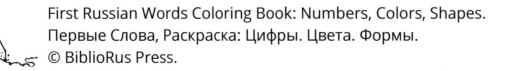

First Russian Words Coloring Book: Numbers, Colors, Shapes.
Первые Слова, Раскраска: Цифры. Цвета. Формы.
© BiblioRus Press.

2

ДВА

[dva]   two

First Russian Words Coloring Book: Numbers, Colors, Shapes.
Первые Слова, Раскраска: Цифры. Цвета. Формы.
© BiblioRus Press.

ТРИ

[tri] three

First Russian Words Coloring Book: Numbers, Colors, Shapes.
Первые Слова, Раскраска: Цифры. Цвета. Формы.

ЧЕТЫРЕ

[chetyre]   four

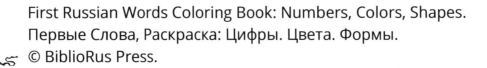

5

ПЯТЬ

[pyat']   five

ШЕСТЬ

[shest']   six

7

СЕМь

[sem']   seven

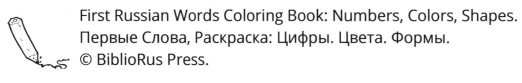

8

ВОСЕМЬ

[vosem']   eight

First Russian Words Coloring Book: Numbers, Colors, Shapes.
Первые Слова, Раскраска: Цифры. Цвета. Формы.
© BiblioRus Press.

9

ДЕВЯТЬ

[devyat']   nine

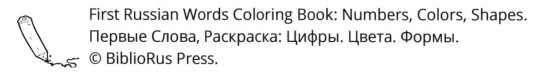First Russian Words Coloring Book: Numbers, Colors, Shapes.
Первые Слова, Раскраска: Цифры. Цвета. Формы.
© BiblioRus Press.

10

ДЕСЯТЬ

[desyat']   ten

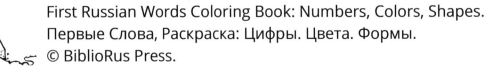

ЦВЕТА

[tsveta]   colors

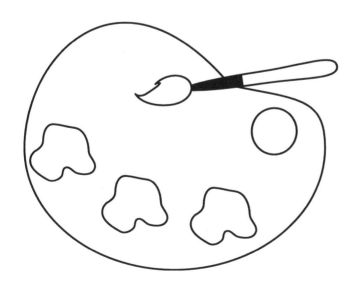

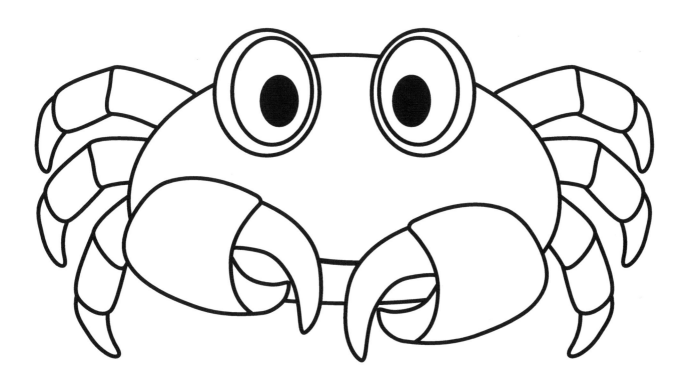

КРАСНЫЙ

[krasniy]   red

First Russian Words Coloring Book: Numbers, Colors, Shapes.
Первые Слова, Раскраска: Цифры. Цвета. Формы.
© BiblioRus Press.

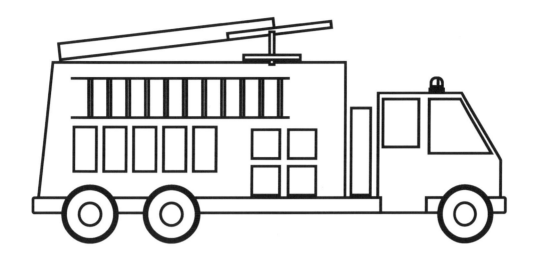

КРАСНЫЙ

[krasniy]   red

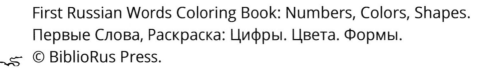

ОРАНЖЕВЫЙ

[oranzheviy]   orange

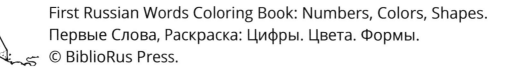

ОРАНЖЕВЫЙ

[oranzheviy]   orange

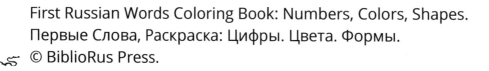

ЖЁЛТЫЙ

[zholtiy]   yellow

ЖЁЛТЫЙ

[zholtiy]　　　　　　　　yellow

First Russian Words Coloring Book: Numbers, Colors, Shapes.
Первые Слова, Раскраска: Цифры. Цвета. Формы.
© BiblioRus Press.

ЗЕЛЁНЫЙ

[zelyoniy]   green

ЗЕЛЁНЫЙ

[zelyoniy]   green

ГОЛУБОЙ

[goluboy]   sky blue

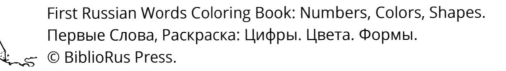

ГОЛУБОЙ

[goluboy]   sky blue

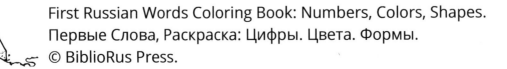

First Russian Words Coloring Book: Numbers, Colors, Shapes.
Первые Слова, Раскраска: Цифры. Цвета. Формы.
© BiblioRus Press.

СИНИЙ

[siniy]   navy blue

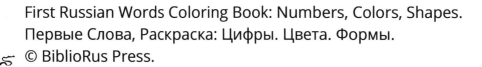

First Russian Words Coloring Book: Numbers, Colors, Shapes.
Первые Слова, Раскраска: Цифры. Цвета. Формы.
© BiblioRus Press.

СИНИЙ

[siniy]   navy blue

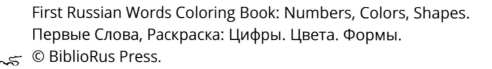

First Russian Words Coloring Book: Numbers, Colors, Shapes.
Первые Слова, Раскраска: Цифры. Цвета. Формы.
© BiblioRus Press.

ФИОЛЕТОВЫЙ

[fioletoviy]   purple

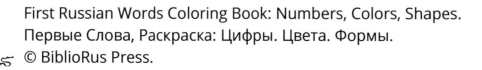

First Russian Words Coloring Book: Numbers, Colors, Shapes.
Первые Слова, Раскраска: Цифры. Цвета. Формы.
© BiblioRus Press.

ФИОЛЕТОВЫЙ

[fioletoviy]   purple

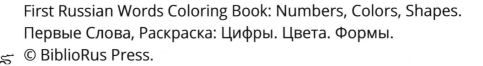

First Russian Words Coloring Book: Numbers, Colors, Shapes.
Первые Слова, Раскраска: Цифры. Цвета. Формы.
© BiblioRus Press.

РОЗОВЫЙ

[rozoviy]   pink

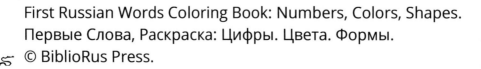

РОЗОВЫЙ

[rozoviy]   pink

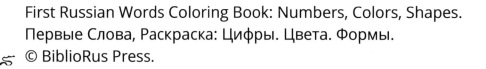

ЧЁРНЫЙ

[chorniy]   black

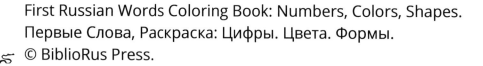

ЧЁРНЫЙ

[chorniy]   black

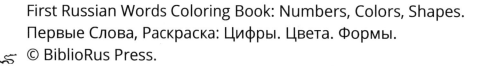

First Russian Words Coloring Book: Numbers, Colors, Shapes.
Первые Слова, Раскраска: Цифры. Цвета. Формы.
© BiblioRus Press.

БЕЛЫЙ

[beliy]   white

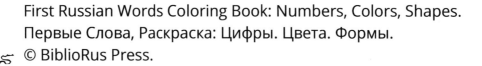

БЕЛЫЙ

[beliy]   white

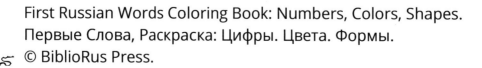

First Russian Words Coloring Book: Numbers, Colors, Shapes.
Первые Слова, Раскраска: Цифры. Цвета. Формы.
© BiblioRus Press.

КОРИЧНЕВЫЙ

[korichneviy]   brown

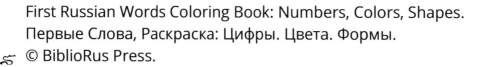

КОРИЧНЕВЫЙ

[korichneviy]   brown

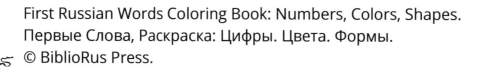

СЕРЫЙ

[seriy]   gray

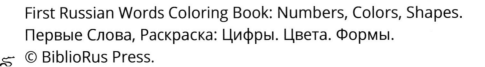

СЕРЫЙ

[seriy]　　　　gray

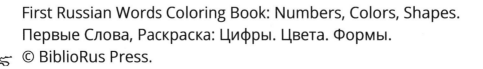

ФОРМЫ

[formy]   shapes

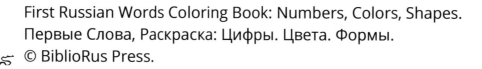

КРУГ

[krug]   circle

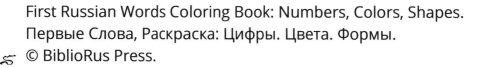

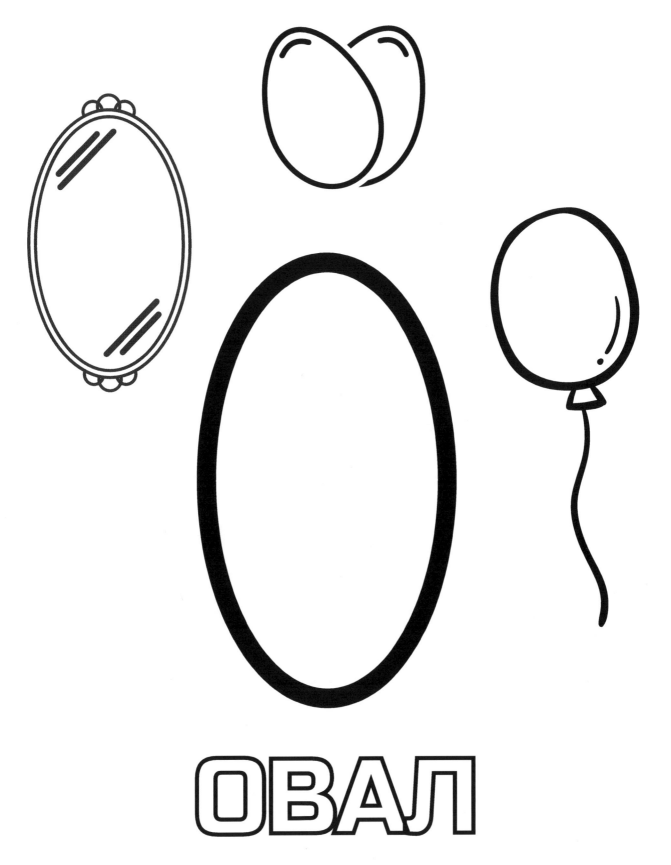

ОВАЛ

[oval]   oval

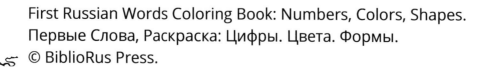

First Russian Words Coloring Book: Numbers, Colors, Shapes.
Первые Слова, Раскраска: Цифры. Цвета. Формы.
© BiblioRus Press.

КВАДРАТ

[kvadrat]　　　　　　　square

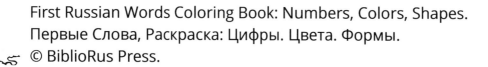

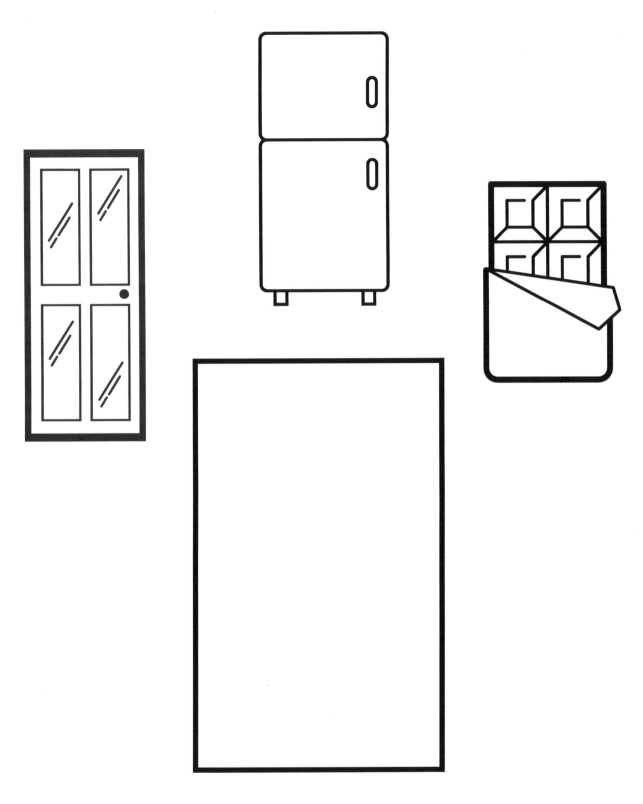

ПРЯМОУГОЛЬНИК

[pryamougol'nik]   rectangle

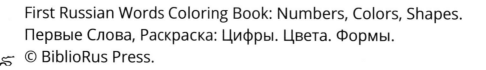

ТРЕУГОЛЬНИК

[treugol'nik]   triangle

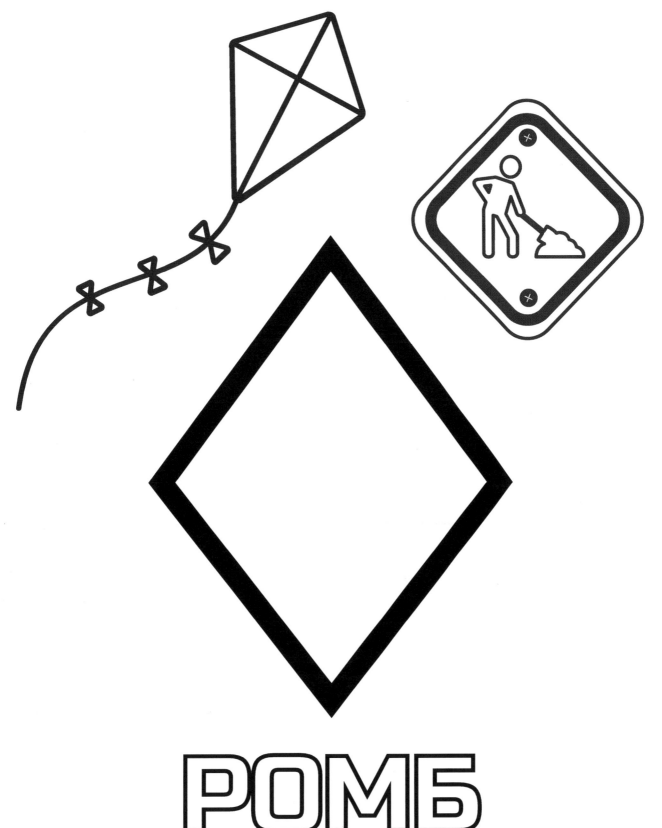

РОМБ

[romb]   diamond

First Russian Words Coloring Book: Numbers, Colors, Shapes.
Первые Слова, Раскраска: Цифры. Цвета. Формы.
© BiblioRus Press.

ЗВЕЗДА

[zvezda]   star

First Russian Words Coloring Book: Numbers, Colors, Shapes.
Первые Слова, Раскраска: Цифры. Цвета. Формы.
© BiblioRus Press.

СЕРДЦЕ

[serdtse]　　　　　　　heart

Made in the USA
Las Vegas, NV
16 December 2024

14455865R00050